# SHAKE
# CATS

## CARLI DAVIDSON

HARPER
DESIGN

*An Imprint of HarperCollins Publishers*

HarperCollins books may be purchased for educational, business,
or sales promotional use. For information please e-mail the
Special Markets Department at SPsales@harpercollins.com.

First published in 2015 by
Harper Design
An Imprint of HarperCollinsPublishers
195 Broadway
New York, NY 10007
Tel: (212) 207-7000
Fax: 855-746-6023
harperdesign@harpercollins.com
www.hc.com

Distributed throughout the world by:
HarperCollinsPublishers
195 Broadway
New York, NY 10007

Library of Congress Control Number: 2015936881
ISBN 978-0-06-235174-6

Printed and bound in China
First Printing, 2015

To all of the people who dedicate their lives to cat rescues and the facilities that support them. In particular the Oregon Humane Society, the Pixie Project, and Panda Paws Rescue all helped greatly in creating this book; thank you for making my art possible.

To Hulk Hogan, my superfierce first cat, a big sexy blond tabby who didn't need balls to be a total badass. Spay and neuter your pets.

And to my sisters Dori, Jeni, and Andi who are also amazing artists and mothers to both humans and animals.

When I was a child, I walked into my local animal shelter and with all the self-assurance of a seven-year-old requested its largest cat. What I really wanted was a tiger, but when I learned the unfortunate truth that my parents were unable to support this dream, I figured I'd settle for the next best thing. That was the day I got my yellow tabby Hulk Hogan—named after my then favorite wrestler.

Hogan, as I liked to call him, wasn't the sort of feline you would want to cross paths with in a dark alley. His face was covered with scars, and at twenty pounds he was all muscle. When I saw him in the shelter, I instantly fell in love with his boldness and independence. He casually walked up to me and smashed his head against my hand, then walked around the room sniffing everything and meowing with a loud, seemingly approving, rumble. His swagger looked more like my dogs' than the more reserved cats I'd met in my neighborhood.

Within a week after moving into our home, he'd single-handedly decimated the bullfrog population in the pond next door, and when he met our eighty-pound boxer, Dempsey, he walked right up to him, spat at him, and batted him across the nose. I'd never seen Dempsey run so fast. Hogan was definitely the undisputed champion of our house.

Hogan was three when I got him and a rescue cat. Like a vast majority of the regal felines you will see in the following pages of this book, he had a life before I met him. He had an established personality and characteristics that I had to learn and take into consideration. He was a scrapper and while he loved affection, he wouldn't approach just anyone. He felt that unattended food was left as a personal offering—even more so than the dogs—and he had an awful fear of cars, which might have kept him off the streets but made it very hard to get him to the vet's office.

People who know me know that I am a huge supporter of adopting animals from shelters, especially older animals, and giving them a second chance. Ask anyone who has ever rescued an animal, and they'll tell you that the appreciation they get from that pet is palpable.

My cats have always been rescues, from my childhood cats, Hogan and Lampshade, the latter was only three pounds of fur and fleas when I took him home, to my current cat, Yushi, who at the moment is head-butting my laptop while I type. They are peers, and I see them as equals. All of my cats taught me lessons that they had learned before we even met. I knew I had a hand in giving them a better life, and they in turn played no small

During the making of *Shake Cats*, I had the opportunity to work with three local Portland animal shelters to find the cat community featured in this book. Most of the cats were living in a shelter when I photographed them, and almost all are rescues. While I was shooting the cats from the shelters, I was also able to provide the shelters with the cats' portraits to help encourage adoption, and a portion of my advance will be donated to all of the shelters that supported this project.

Additionally, some of the cats featured in this book are either diabetic or FIV+. Both are conditions that some people think require a lot of money and time to take care of, so many of these cats don't get adopted. However, what many people don't know is that both of these health conditions are easily manageable through a controlled diet and medication.

While my beloved childhood feline companion Hogan hailed from an era when indoor and outdoor cats were all the rage, I have since become a huge proponent of indoor-only cats. This stems partly from the fact that cats are skilled predators that often hunt native wildlife. As a strong supporter of conserving a safe environment for native species, I've let go of the idea that cats can be happy only with access to the outdoors. Instead, I've created an indoor environment that lets my cat hunt less established creatures, like catnip-filled bananas and neon-pink stuffed mice. My cat roommate, Yushi, doesn't seem unhappy with her selection of prey, and when it's nice out she has a leash and harness so we can hang outside together. The other reason why I support indoor-only cats is because when I was fifteen I lost my amazing and beautiful cat friend Lampshade to a hit-and-run accident.

I cannot stress enough the importance of adopting, neutering, and spaying cats. According to the ASPCA, on average in the United States 1.4 MILLION cats will be euthanized every year due to pet overpopulation. Even with the extensive shelter system in the U.S., only 37 percent of cats in shelters are adopted compared to the 41 percent that are euthanized. By spaying and neutering your pet, or helping a friend in financial need get their own pet sterilized, you are preventing needless suffering and helping create more resources for the animals already in shelters. There are often low-cost surgeries available, so you should reach out to your local shelters for details. Animals who are fixed mark significantly less or not at all, have more docile temperaments, and tend to live longer. Also, many cancers of the reproductive organs and mammary glands are avoided with spaying and neutering.

After having worked with such an incredible and diverse range of cats, I'm reminded that as humans we are left with the responsibility to make sure they have a place as well as a voice in our society. I ask that you consider adopting a rescue the next time you're looking to open your home to a new pet, and I implore you to consider an older, diabetic, or FIV+ cat for your next companion.

—*Carli Davidson*

# HOW DID I GET THE CATS TO SHAKE?

Growing up with Hogan taught me so much about how to listen to my instincts when it came to handling animals, especially tough felines like him. We climbed trees together and stalked around my back yard pouncing on leaves. However, the most important lesson I learned from that fierce tabby was knowing when, and when not, to pet a cat simply by reading its body language—a knowledge I've applied to almost every species of animal I've worked with since.

Working with cats for this book was exciting, but definitely different from working with dogs. I was slightly worried that I would have a lot of fearful cats I couldn't work with. Part of this stemmed from Hulk Hogan's absolute hatred of riding in cars, because any time we'd put him in a crate he'd poop and then roll in it.

To my surprise, I discovered that most cats were actually enriched by the experience. When they first arrived at the studio, we'd open their crates and let them explore the space. Some would hide for a while under a gear shelf or behind rolls of photography paper, but most went straight to the piles of treats we had around the studio. By the end of the session, many of the cats were casually walking around the studio; some were even jumping in my lap while I was editing their photos. It's amazing what you can achieve with some catnip and a laser pointer.

Like with *Shake* and *Shake Puppies*, all of the models were different and required their own style of handling. Some cats fell asleep on the staging table under the warm glow of the modeling lights, some were so motivated by food they almost took our fingers off while snatching the treats from our hands, and some saw one flash of the light, hissed at me, and showed themselves to the door—an action we jokingly came to refer to as "the cat middle finger."

Since the release of my first two books, many people have asked me how I get the animals to shake. I feel with cats it's important to share how I did it since it could come across as cruel if people assumed I was simply dumping water on them. In the beginning, we experimented with a few different approaches. Although we never sprayed the cats directly with water, my assistants and I did get them wet slowly by putting a bit of water in our hands and petting their fur. However, the best way I found to get the cats to shake was more of a grooming process.

Full disclosure, I hired an animal care professional to help me with this, and I do not recommend you try it without one for the health and safety of your pets. I had a professional vet tech and another animal care specialist help me give the cats an ear cleaning—for some, a much needed ear cleaning with Epi-Otic ear cleaner, not water—and a nail trim. Since I worked in animal care for close to a decade and have cleaned more ears than I can count I assisted them as well. The ear cleaning was to solicit the shake. The nail trim was just a thank you to the owners and shelter workers who sacrificed their time to bring in their cats for me to photograph. Though some cats' ears stay very clean, many still need a flush now and again for dirt, wax, and ear mites, so keep an eye on your cat's ear health.

While the cats were not always huge fans of their brief cleaning session, they were generally quick to forgive in exchange for some love and affection, especially the rescue cats, who were pretty desensitized to new people and things either due to living on the streets or just because of the bustle of shelter life. Being around so many cats was fascinating. I think it's easy to forget how unique cats can be, especially since we don't run into them socially as we do with dogs being walked in parks or on sidewalks. Working on this book, I was reminded of how varied and tender their personalities are.

# MODELS

Thank you so much to everyone who took the time to come to my studio or welcome me into your animal shelter, and who trusted your cats to my vision. I am endlessly impressed by how the Portland-area community comes together to provide me with such amazing variety. None of the cats in this book are "professional models" (but don't let my cat, Yushi, know I said that or she may pee on my favorite sweater). They were all sourced from friends, rescue groups, and social media.

The following are the cat models by order of appearance:

Rescue 1

Finnik

Jaz

Binx

Lorax

Ginger

Rescue 2

Rescue 3

Katie

Big Ben

Gandolf

Rescue 4

Grandpaw

Gomesia OEB

Maurice

Eywa

Rescue 5

Regulator

Rescue 6    Arkham    Darius    Malcolm    Tickles    Rescue 7

Squishy    Rescue 8    Yushi    Lil Bub    Quincy    Diego

Frankie    Amber    Rescue 9    Beyonce    Rescue 10    Otis

Marti    Abby    Tellele    Tom    Rescue 11    Penny

 ChiCheeLina

 Blue

 Rescue 12

 Kiki

 Ozzy

 Greta

 Snuggs

 Freyja

 Sitka

 Sherlock

 Tiny Cat

 Dandelion

 Mango

 Rescue 13

 Mushy

 Jet

 Maybel

 Cal

 Meghan

# ACKNOWLEDGMENTS

This book called for some seriously crazy cat ladies to get onboard my crew! To that point, I'd like to thank the queen of cat whisperers, Tanya Paul, and her almost psychic connection with all felines. Also, of course, Amanda Giese, who reached out to rescues, shelters, and owners. She found most of the cats in these pages, assisted handling them in the studio, and helped build a bridge with the amazing animal adoption megateam at the Oregon Humane Society, which includes Barbara Baugnon and Jennifer Barta. To Amy Sacks at the Pixie Project, thank you for all your support and access to your adorable kittens. Also thank you to Meghan Murphy and Bree Winchell for helping out on set as well!

My agent, Jean Sagendorph, another cat lady in my life, who has helped make so many cool projects possible for me since we first met through Kuo-Yu Liang. Thanks again to both of you!

My insightful editor, Paige Doscher, a woman who loves cats to a fault. Even though she is allergic to them, she still convinced her parents to adopt one when she was a kid.

Tim Wiesch, the craziest cat dude of them all and Yushi's favorite human who cooks amazing meals, makes knives, writes comics, can fix anything, mows our too-big lawn every weekend, keeps my messes semi-contained, and is pretty much a superhuman.

To all the women who make art.

For bringing me endless joy and entertainment: Andi Davidson, Michael Rudin, Joanne Kim, Gio Marcus, Holly Andres, Michael Durham, Sierra Hahn, Joseph Russo, Chuck Davidson, Deena Davidson, Jennifer Harris, Dori Johnson, Leslie Davidson, Danielle Davidson, Andrew Davidson, all the Wiesches and kin (Meghan, Marti, Brett, Katie, Maeve, Jake, Billy, Lucas, Eric, Joey, Zack, and Maddy), Joe Preston, Eric Powell, Alana DaFonseca, Danica Anderson, Hukee, Ryan Hill, Carlos Donahue, Janice Moses, Cheyanne Allott, Sarah Grace McCandless, Lance Kreiter, Krisi Rose, Seth Casteel, Mike & Bub, the Finks, Erica Diehl, Michelle Borges, Dylan Benadi, Hannah Ingram, Craig Thompson, Scott Harrison, Jen Lin, Marcus and Ro, Stephanie Lundin, Ali Skiba, Glynis Olsen, Nikon Cameras, the crew at Variable, Pushdot Studios, my team at HarperCollins (Liz Esman, Renata Marchione, Penny Makras, Lynne Yeamans, and Marta Schooler), Gary, Beast, and Jade. Most of all, to the shelters who opened their doors to me out of a place of trust and mutual respect, and to the pet owners who took the time to bring their cats into the studio as models for this book.

Special thanks to Regulator, my first ever shake cat. He was an epic model, friend, against-all-odds rescue, and living deity. Rest in peace, buddy!